We Like

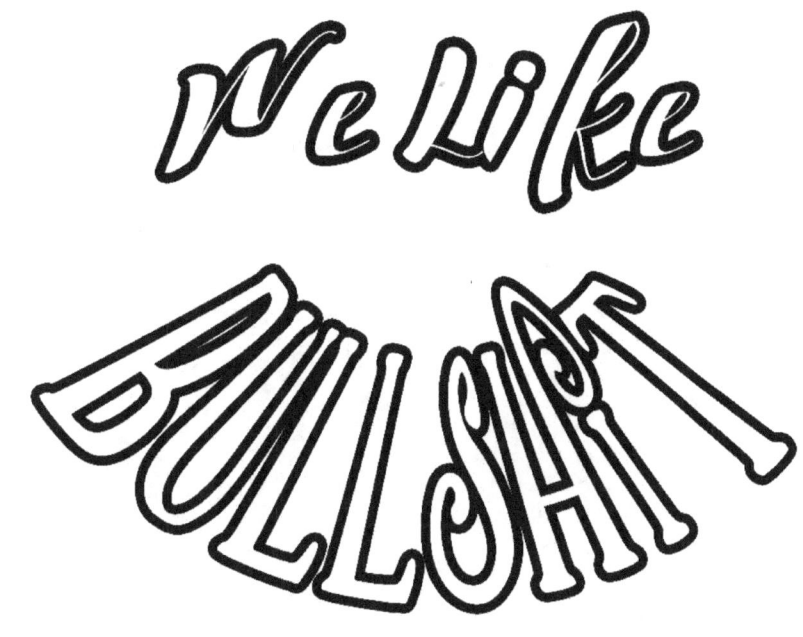
BULLSHIT

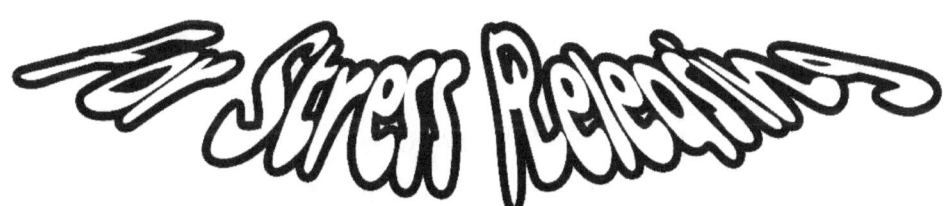
Brilliant Swear Word To Color

For Stress Releasing

Bear Smith Idiot

Happy Coloring!

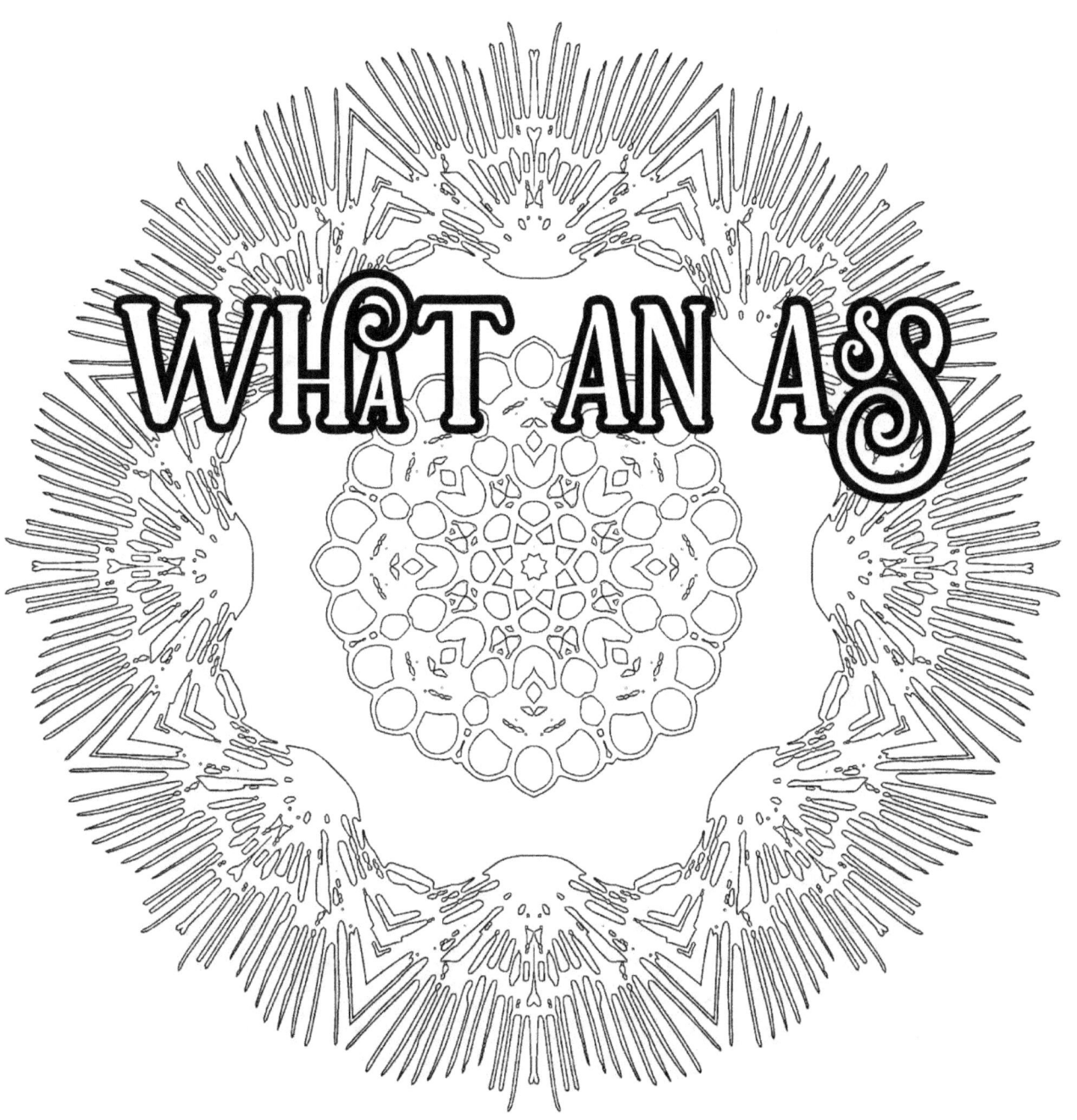

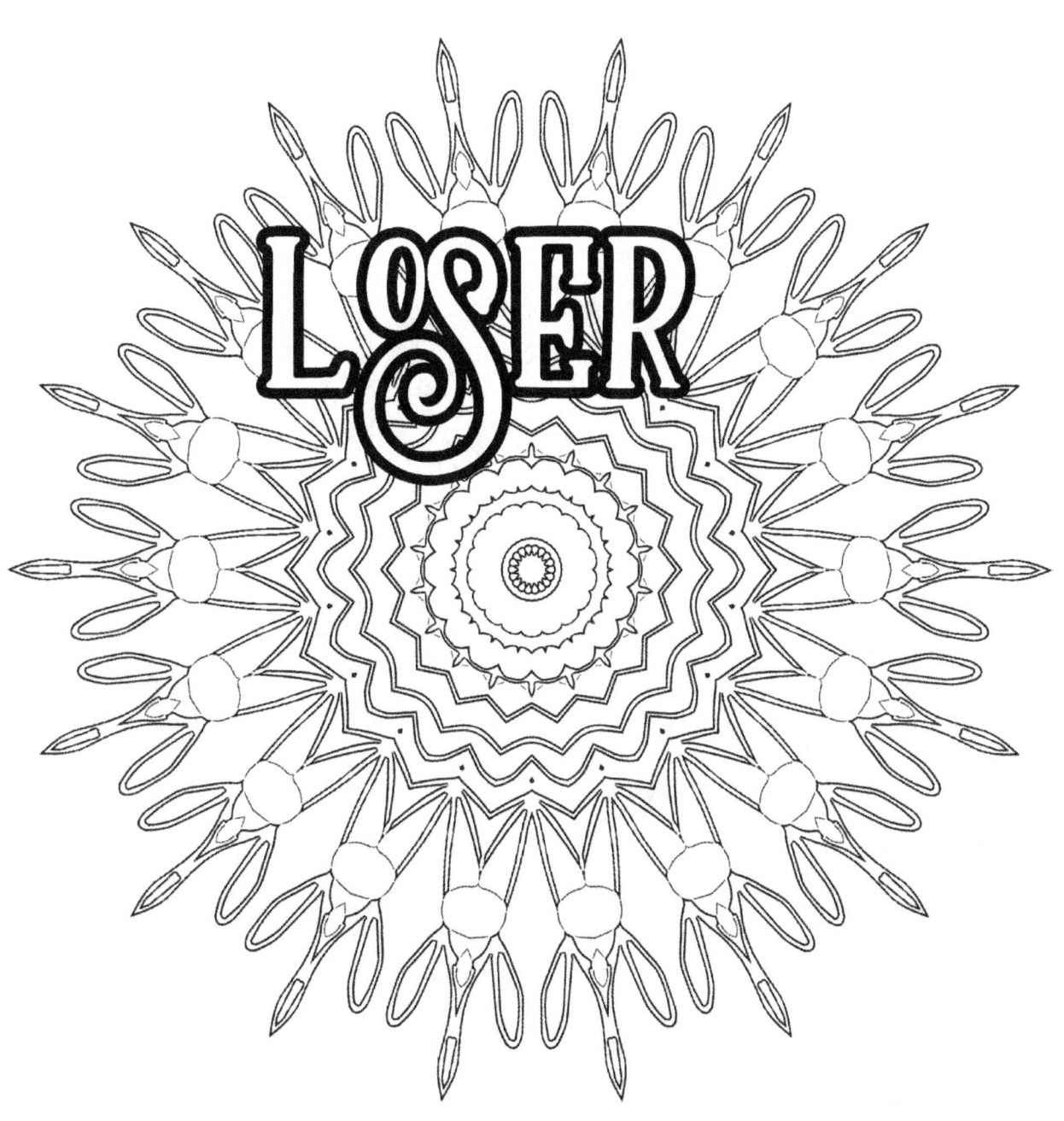

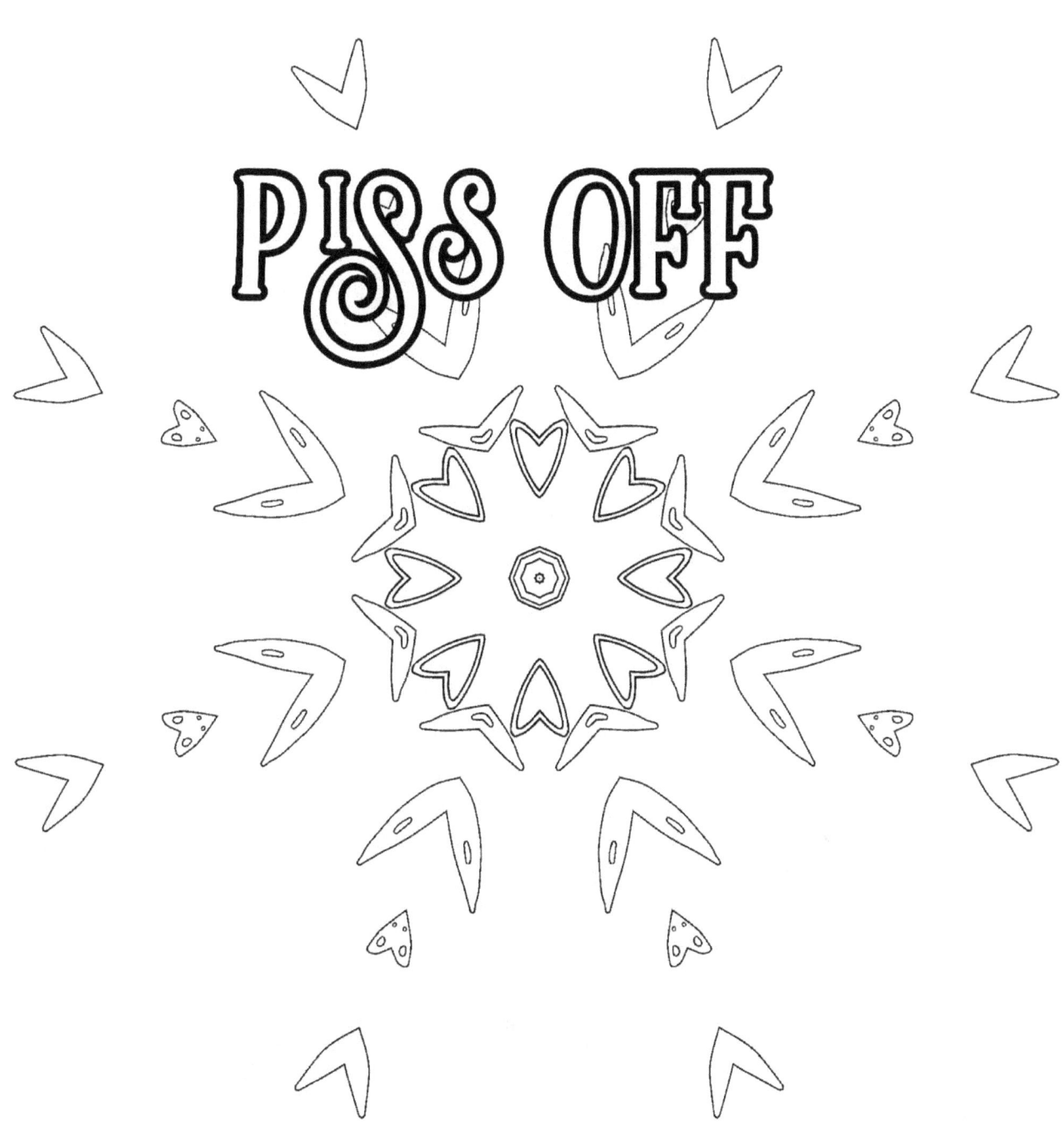

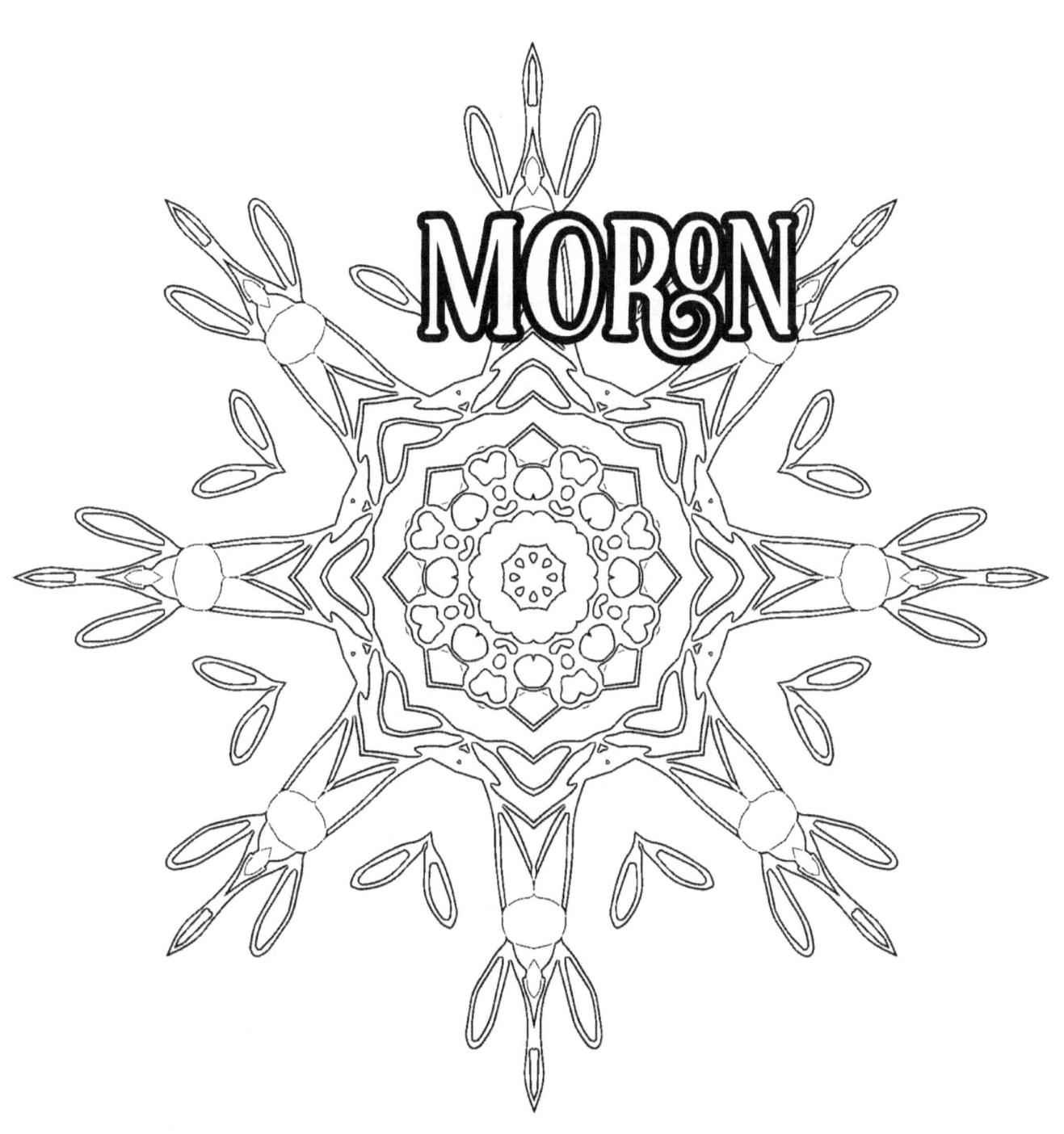

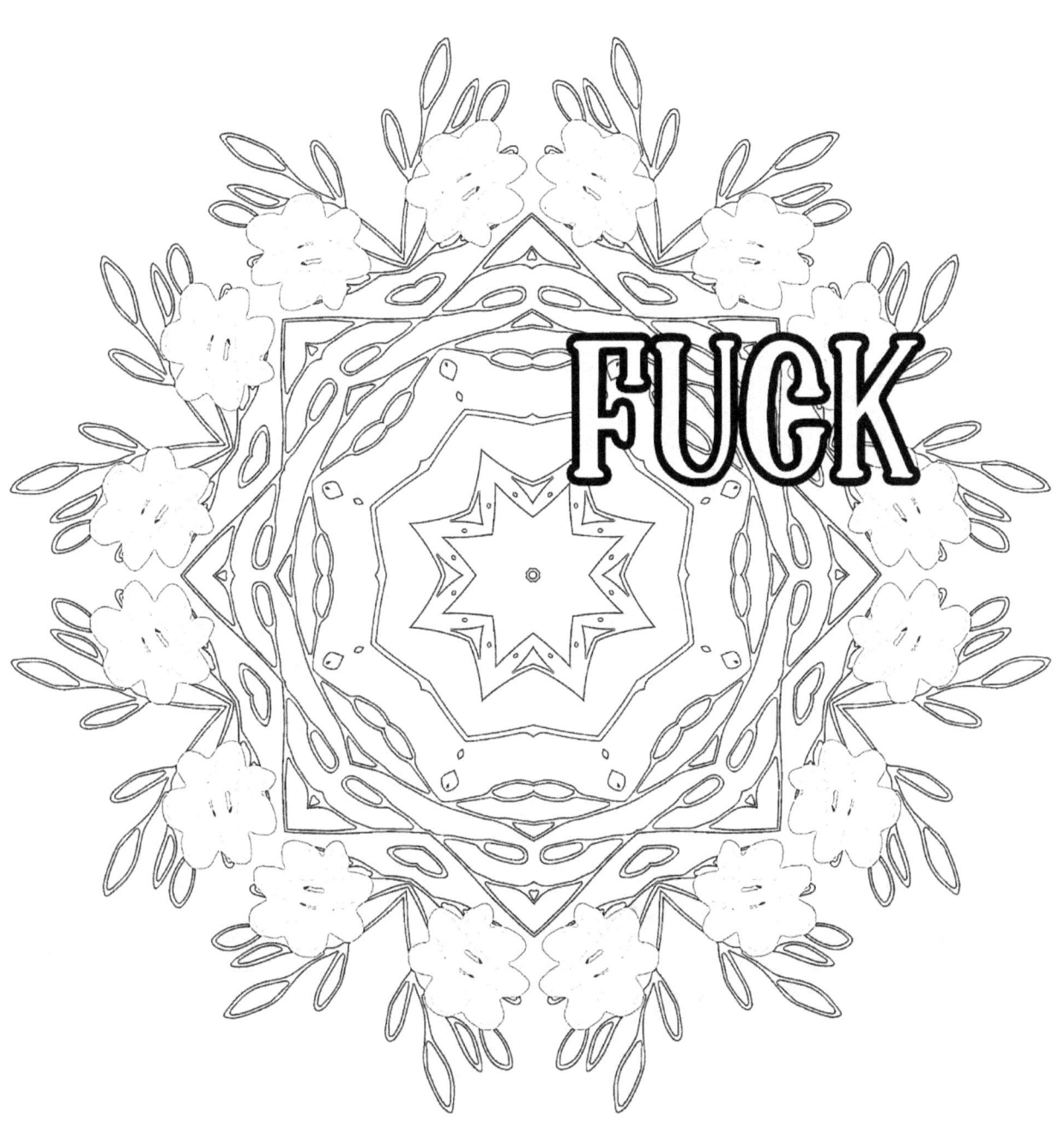

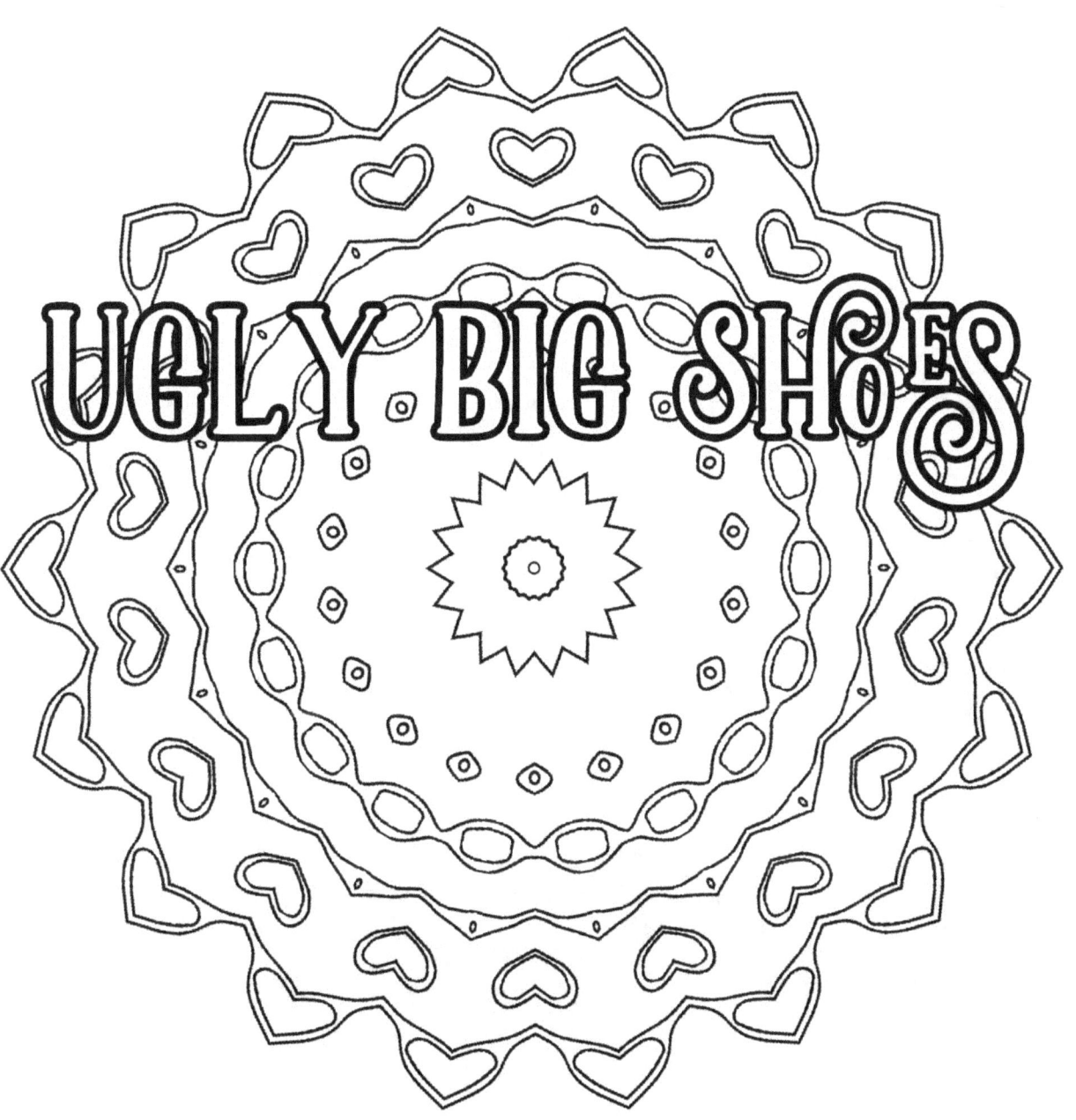

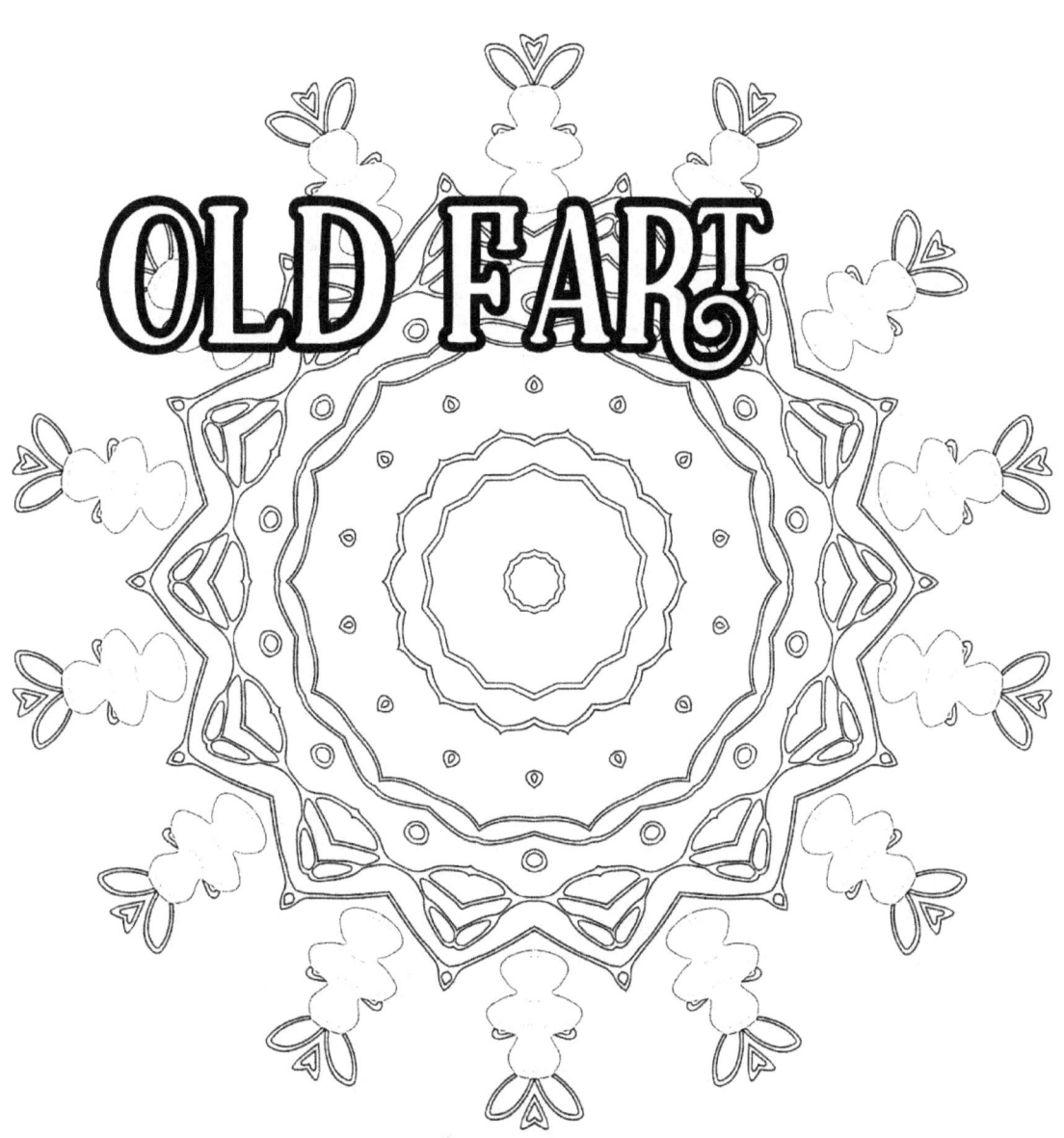

OLD FART

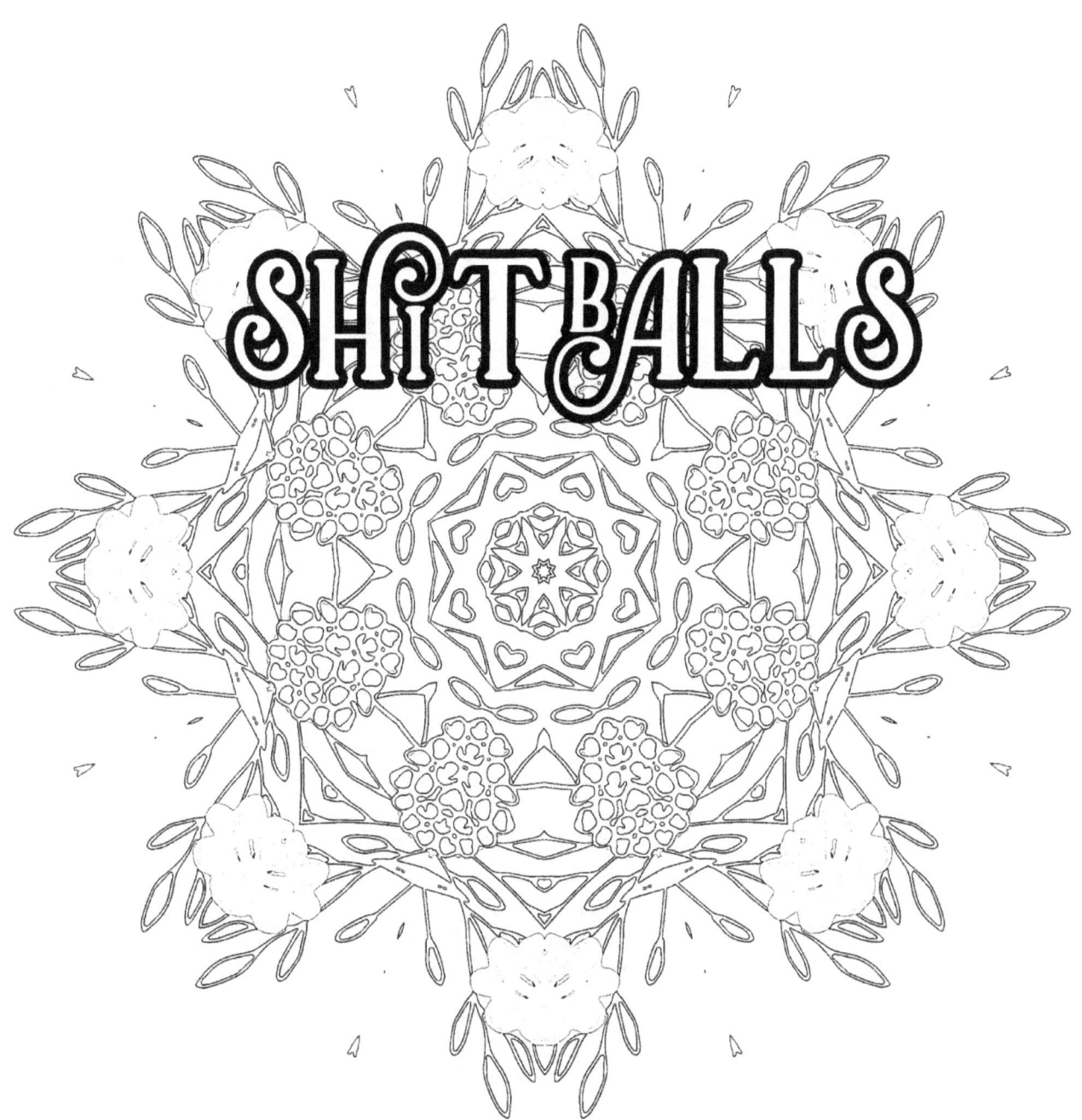

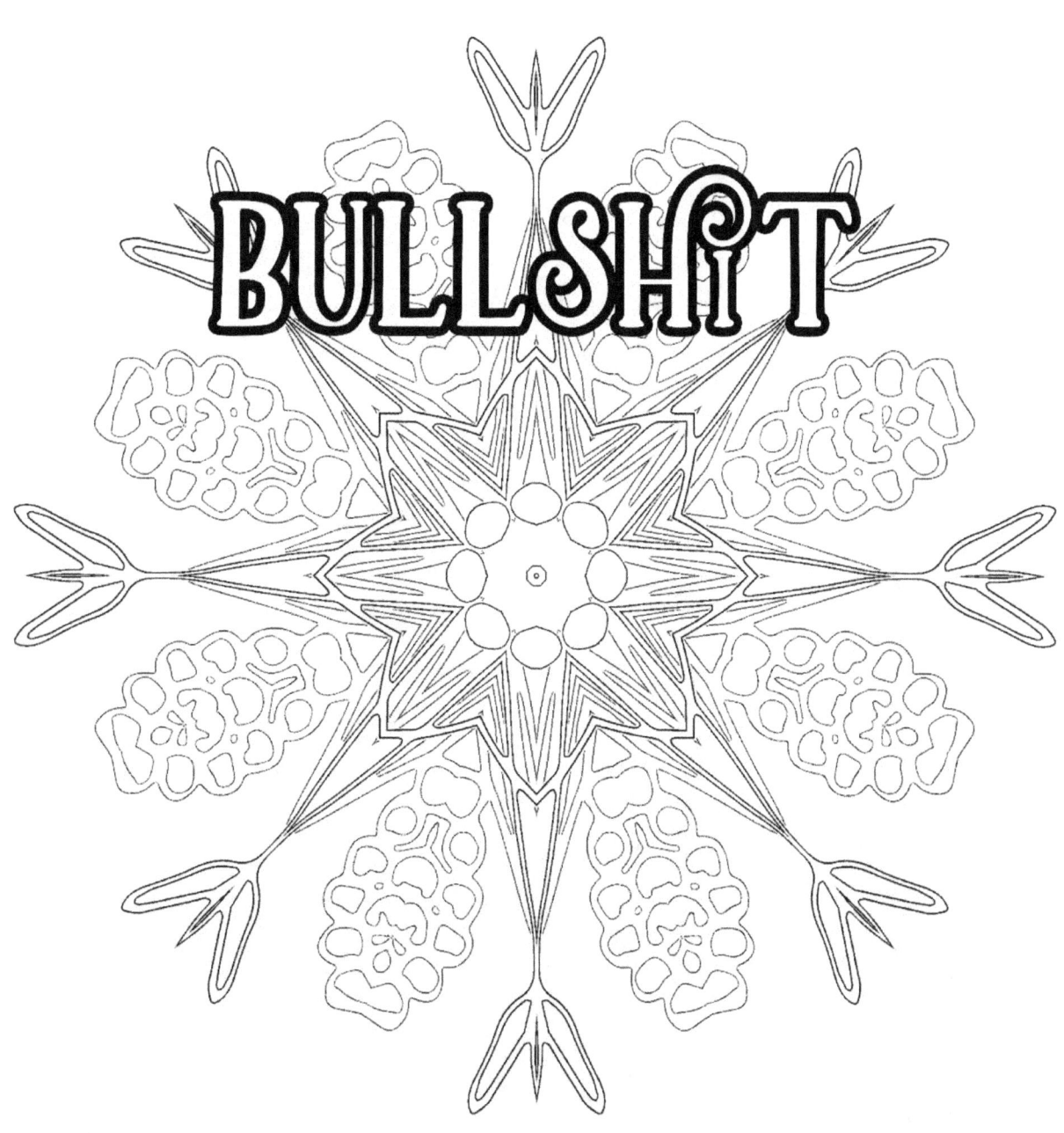

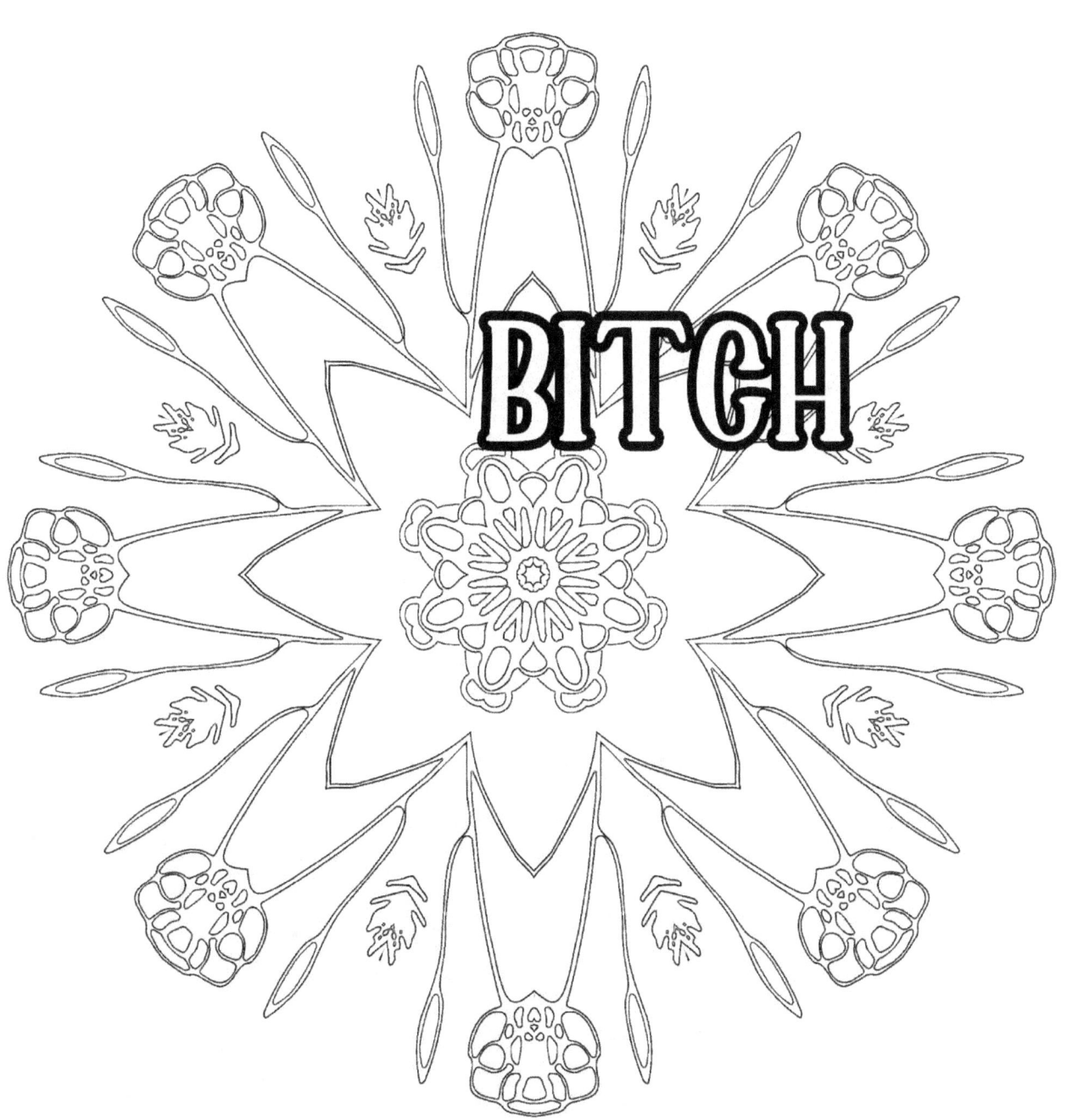

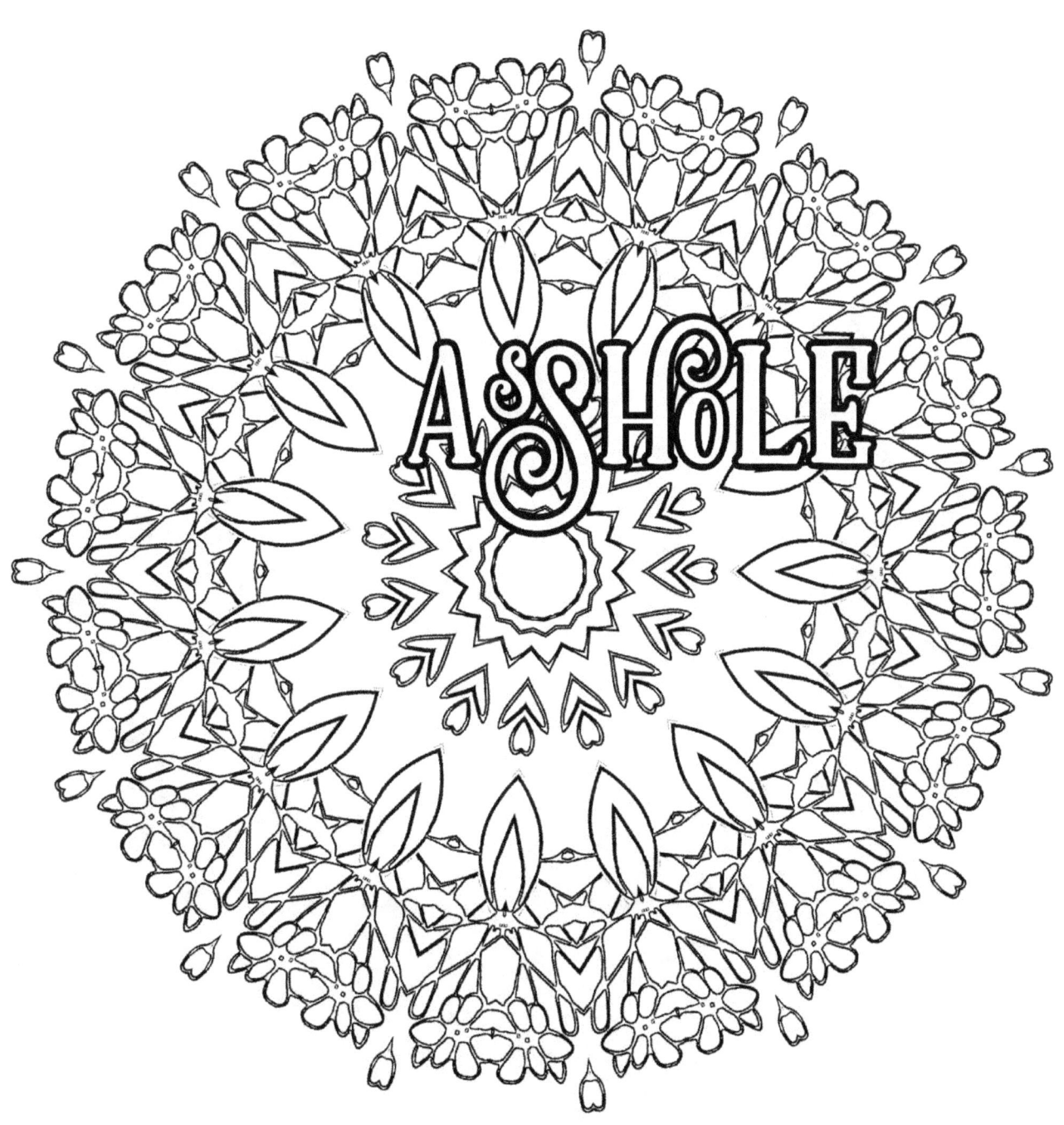

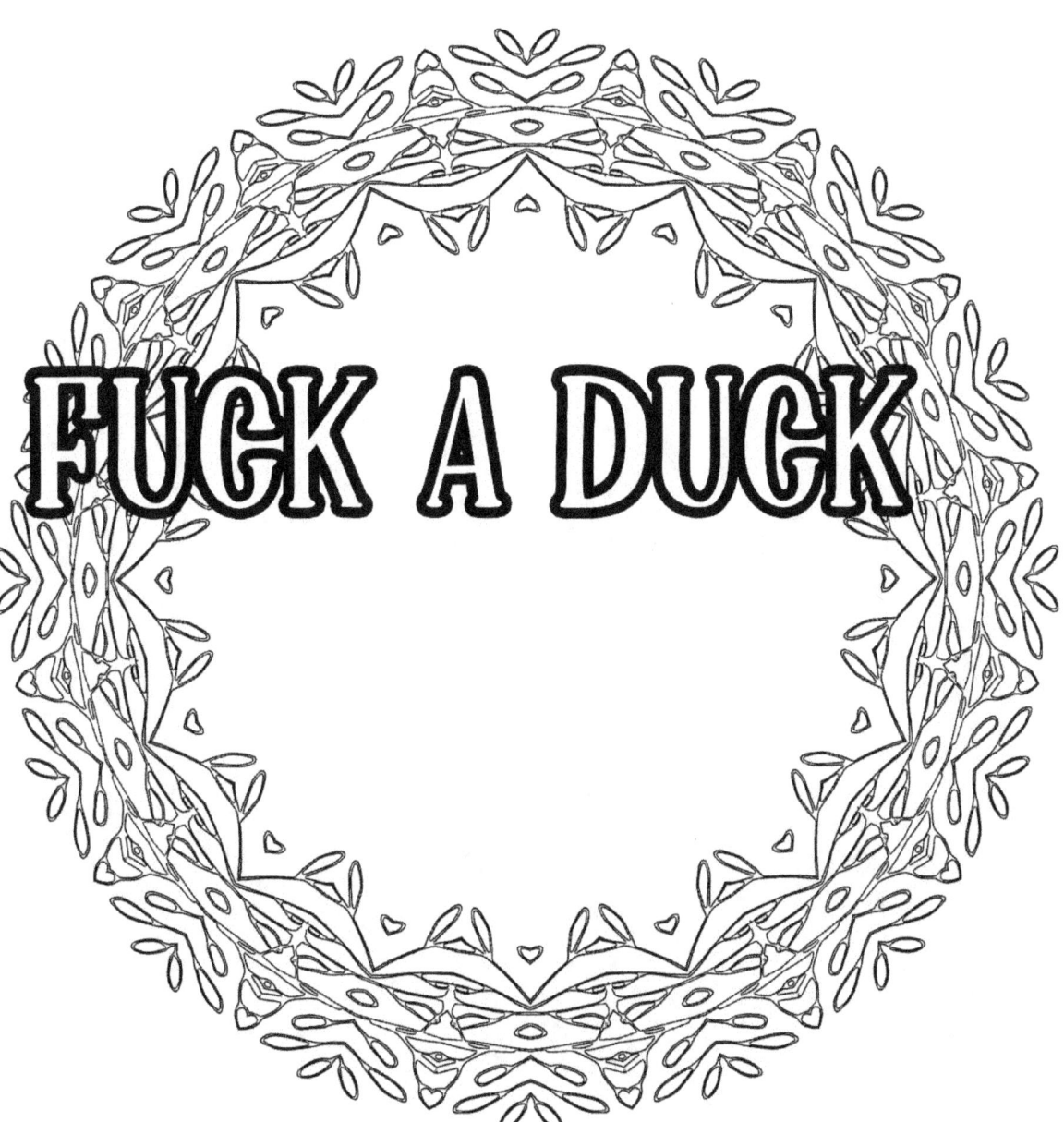

FUCK A DUCK

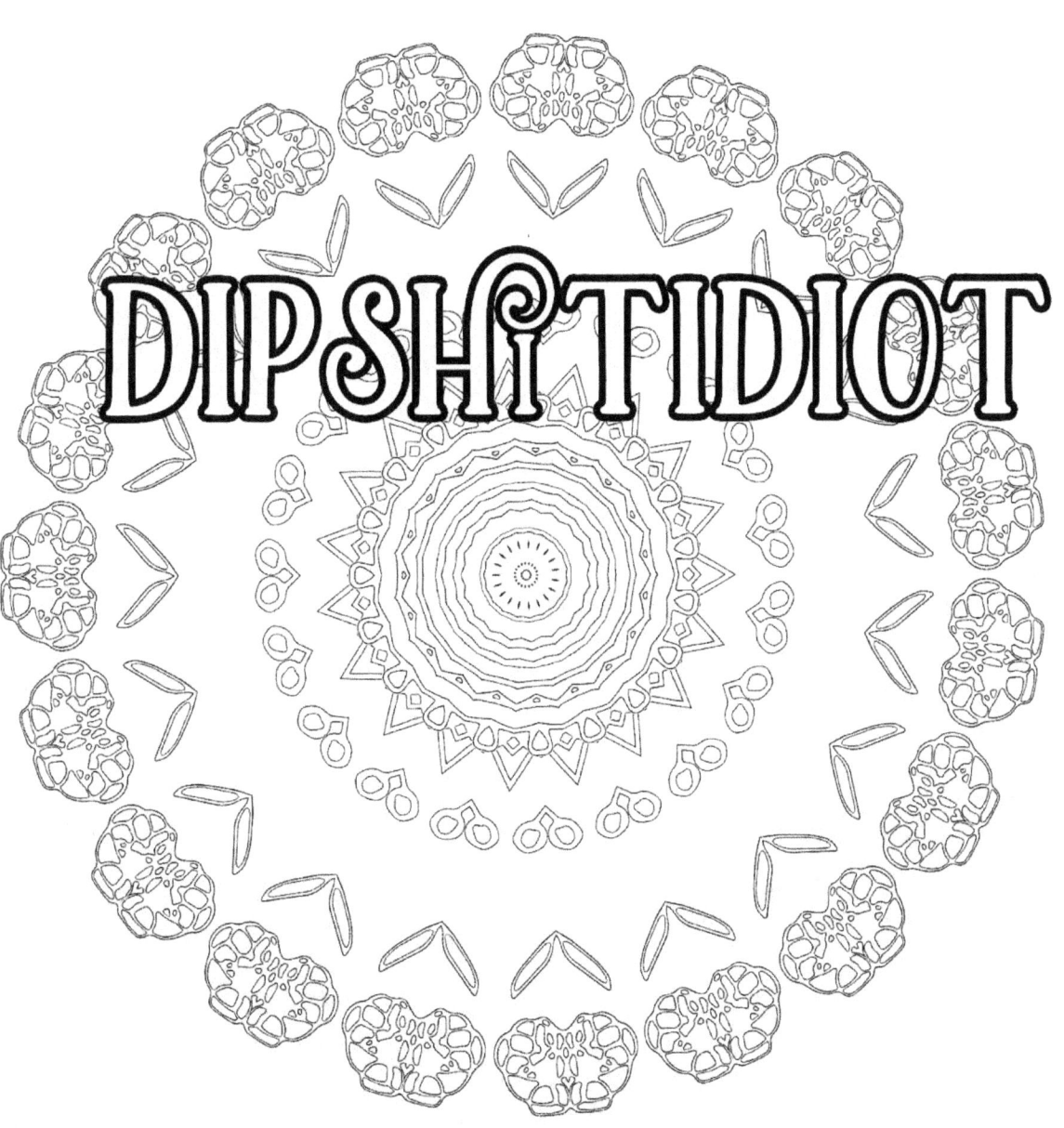

DIPSHIT IDIOT

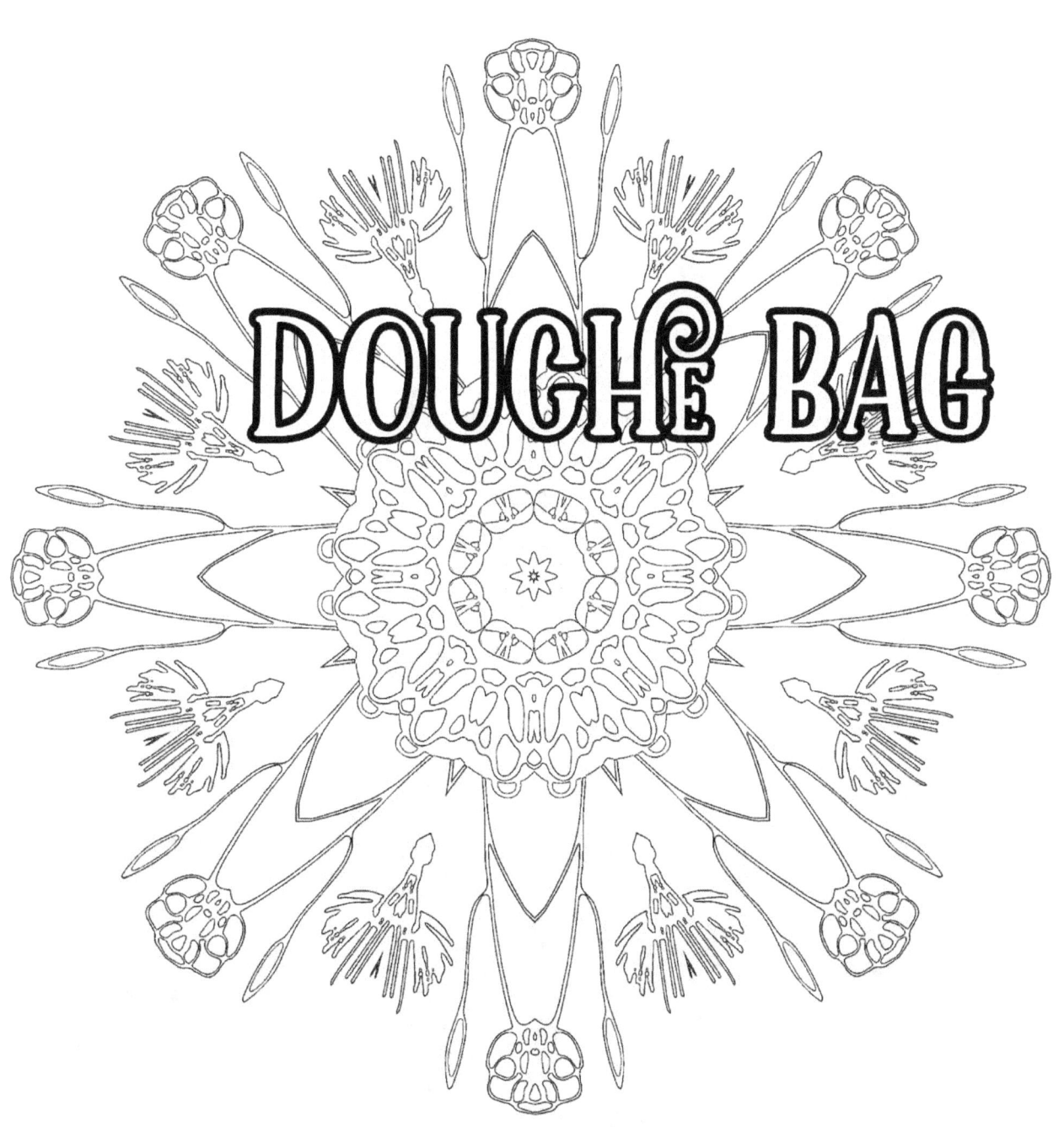

DOUCHE BAG

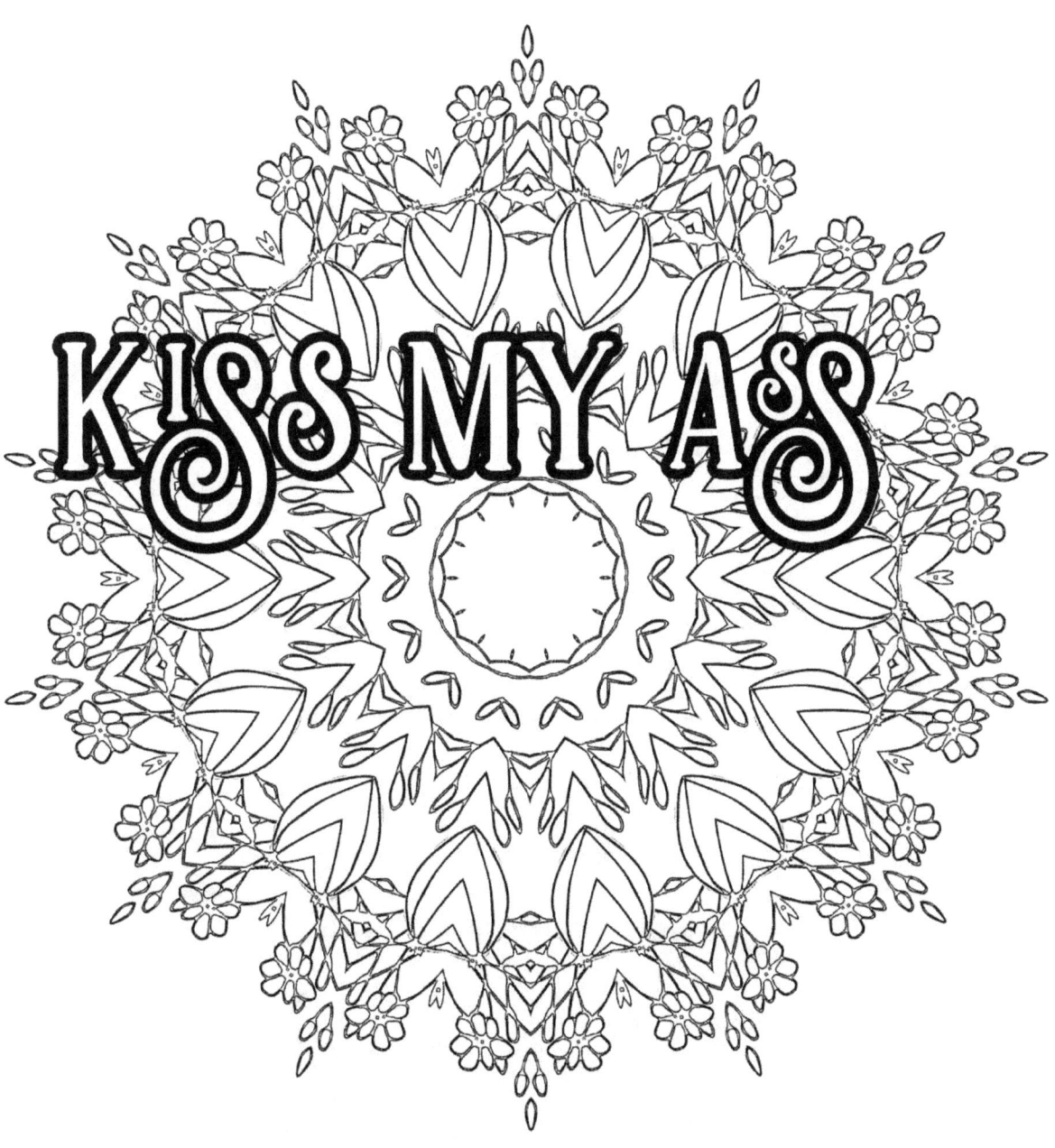

DICKHEAD

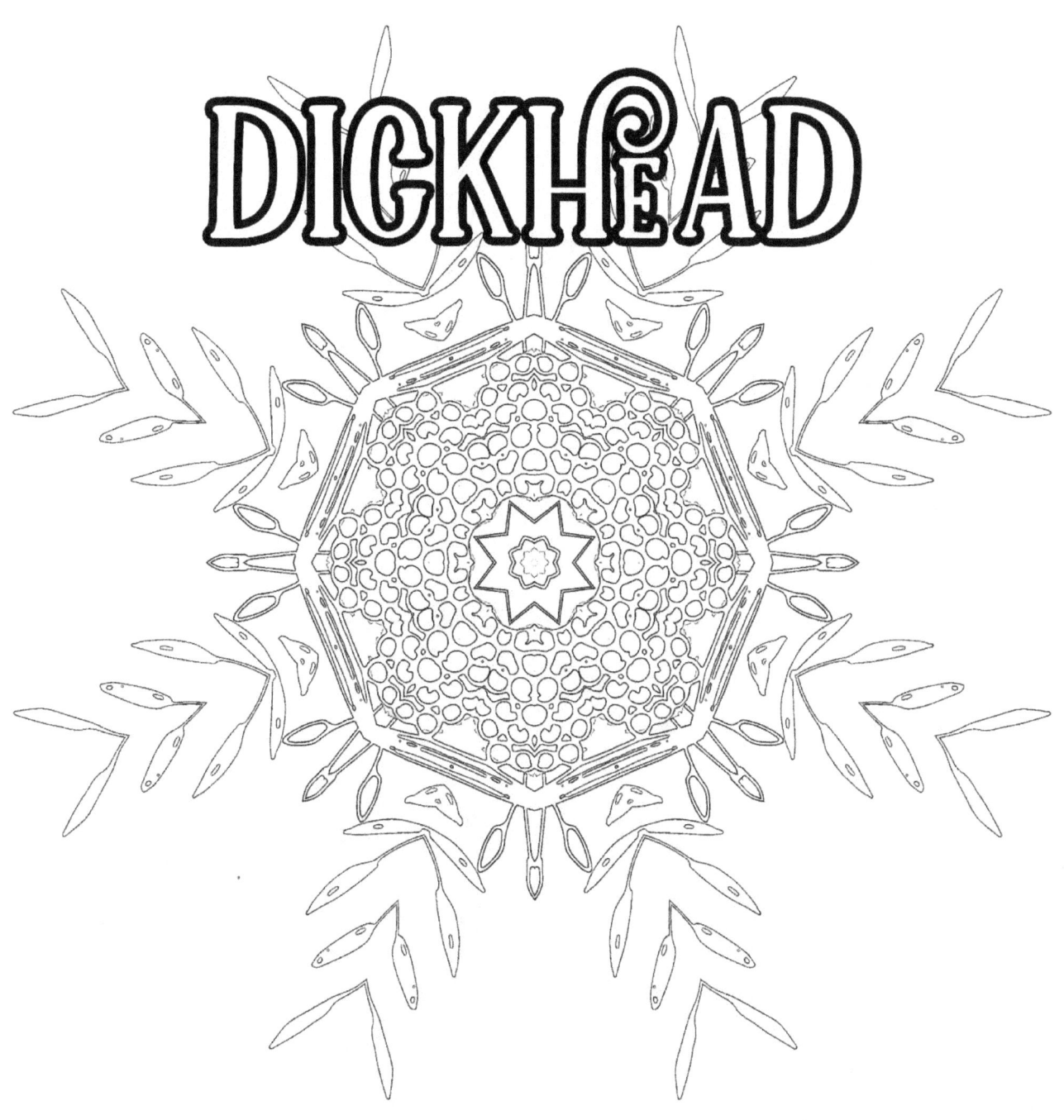

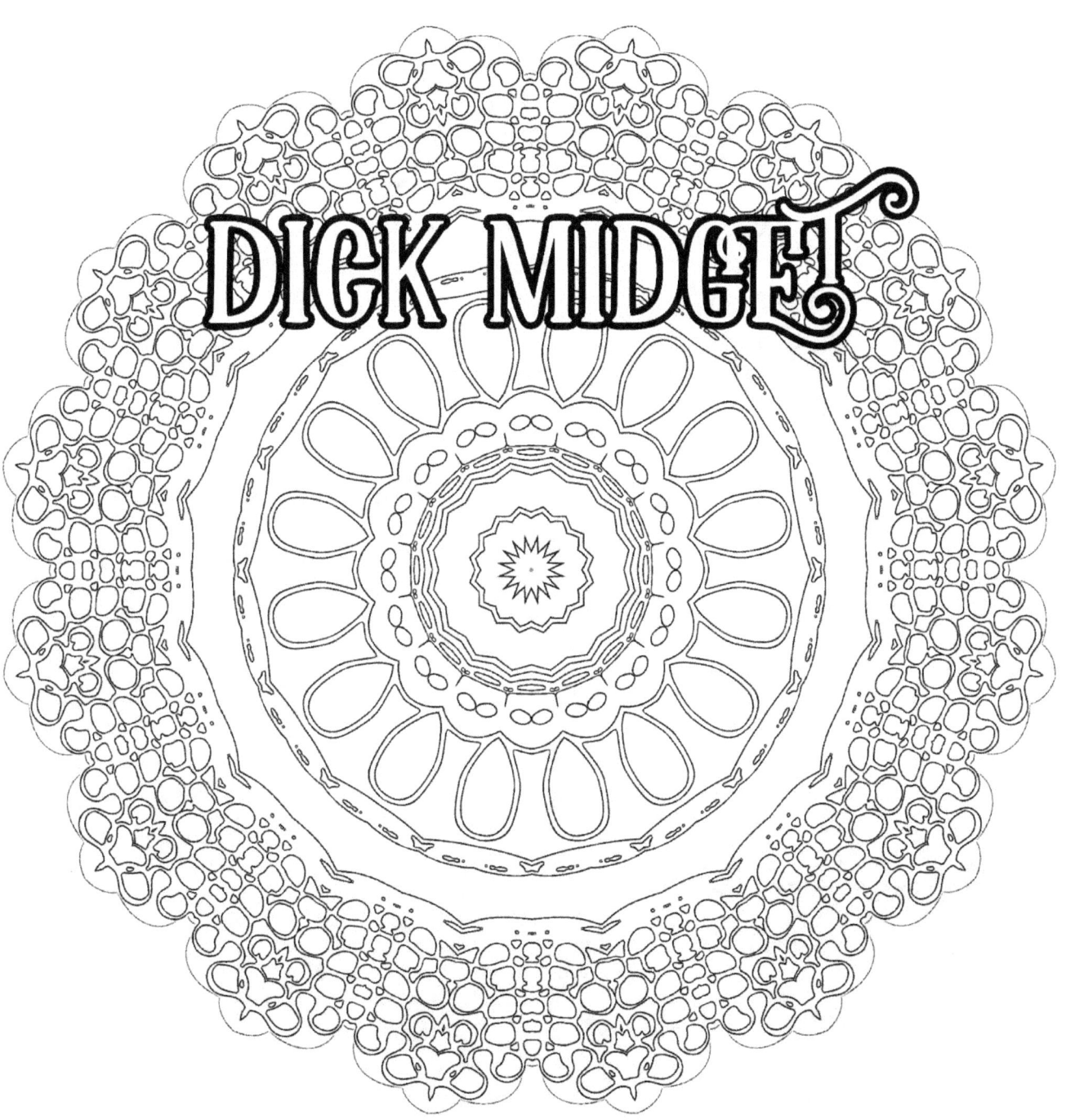

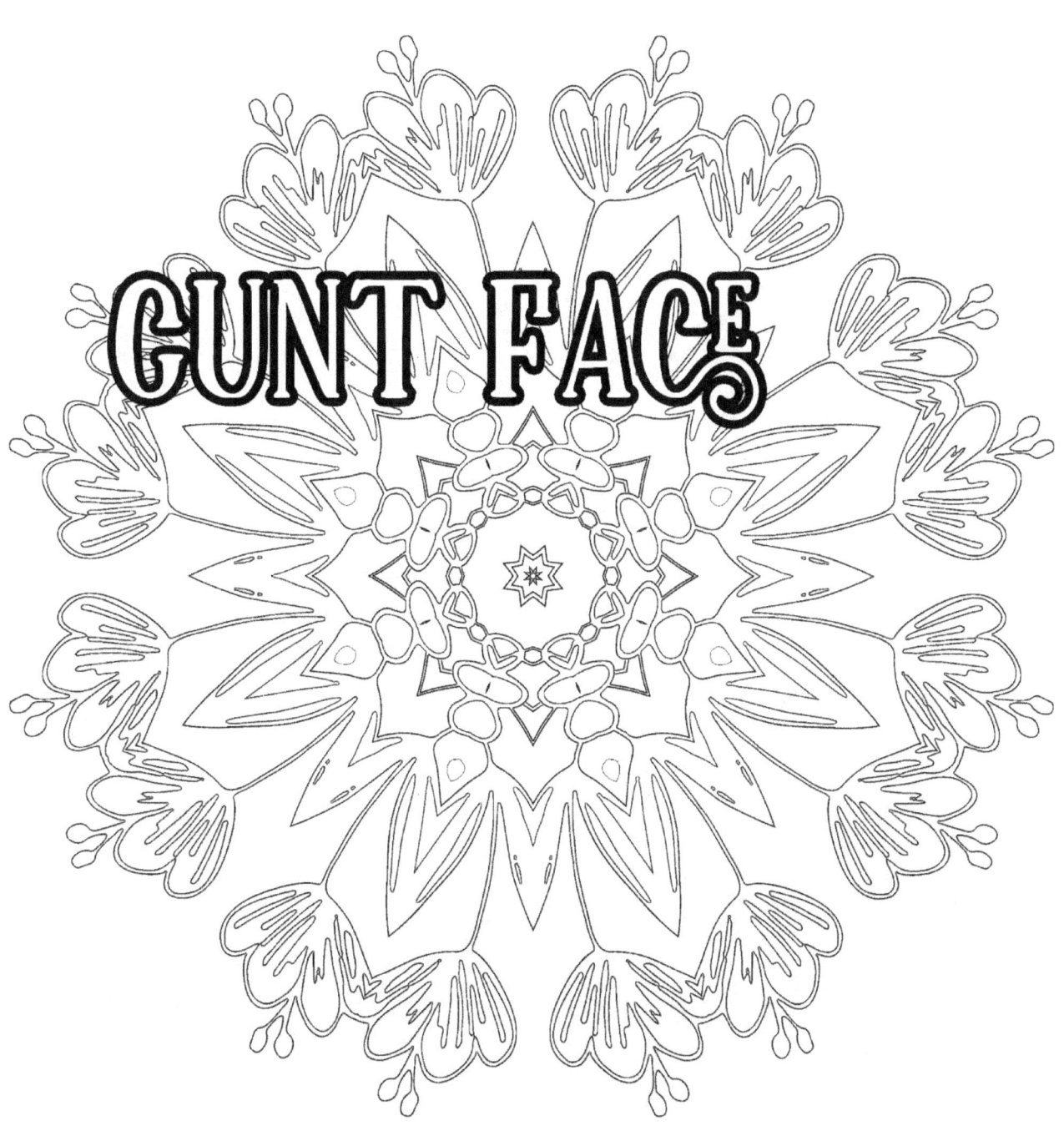

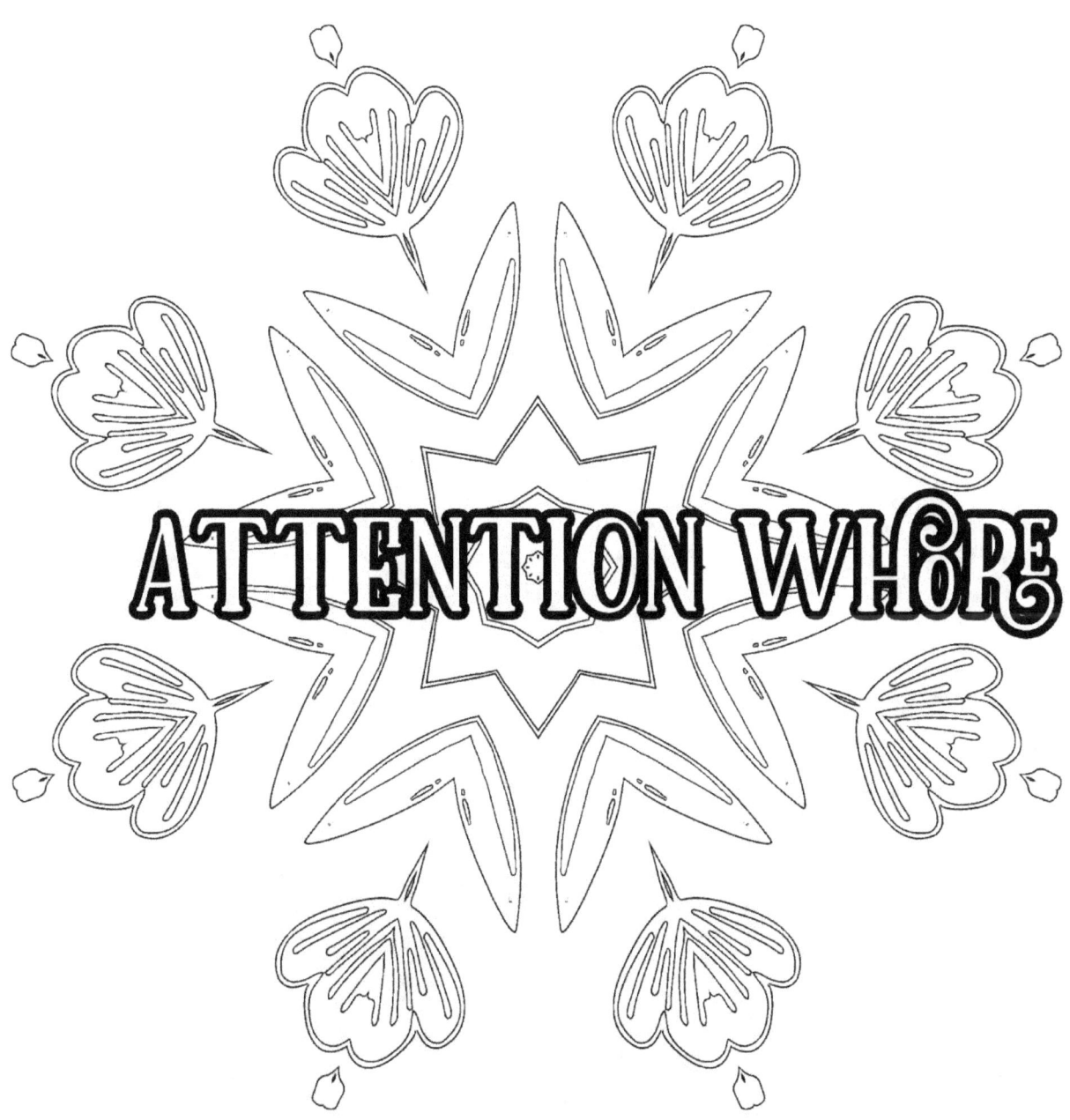

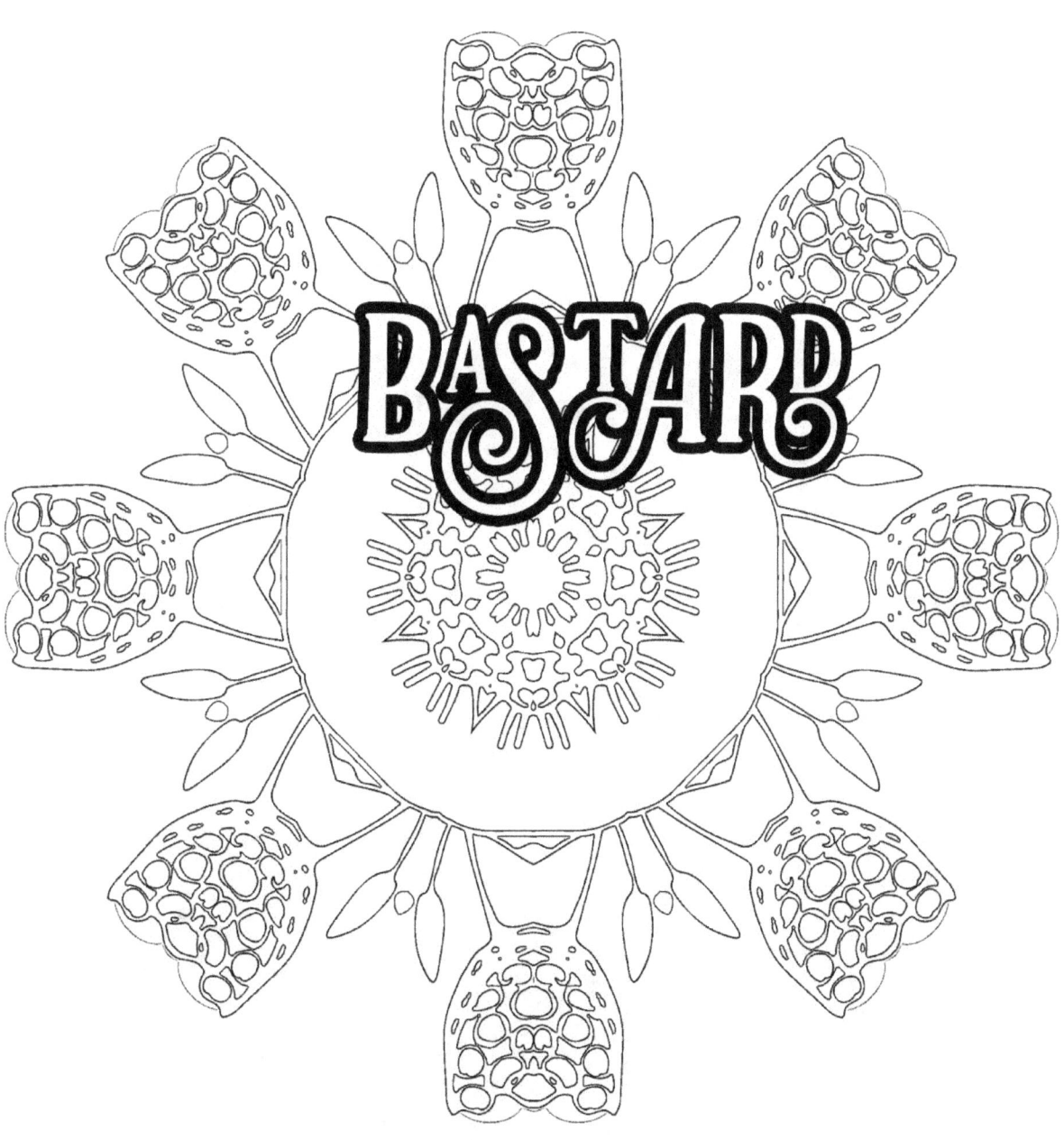

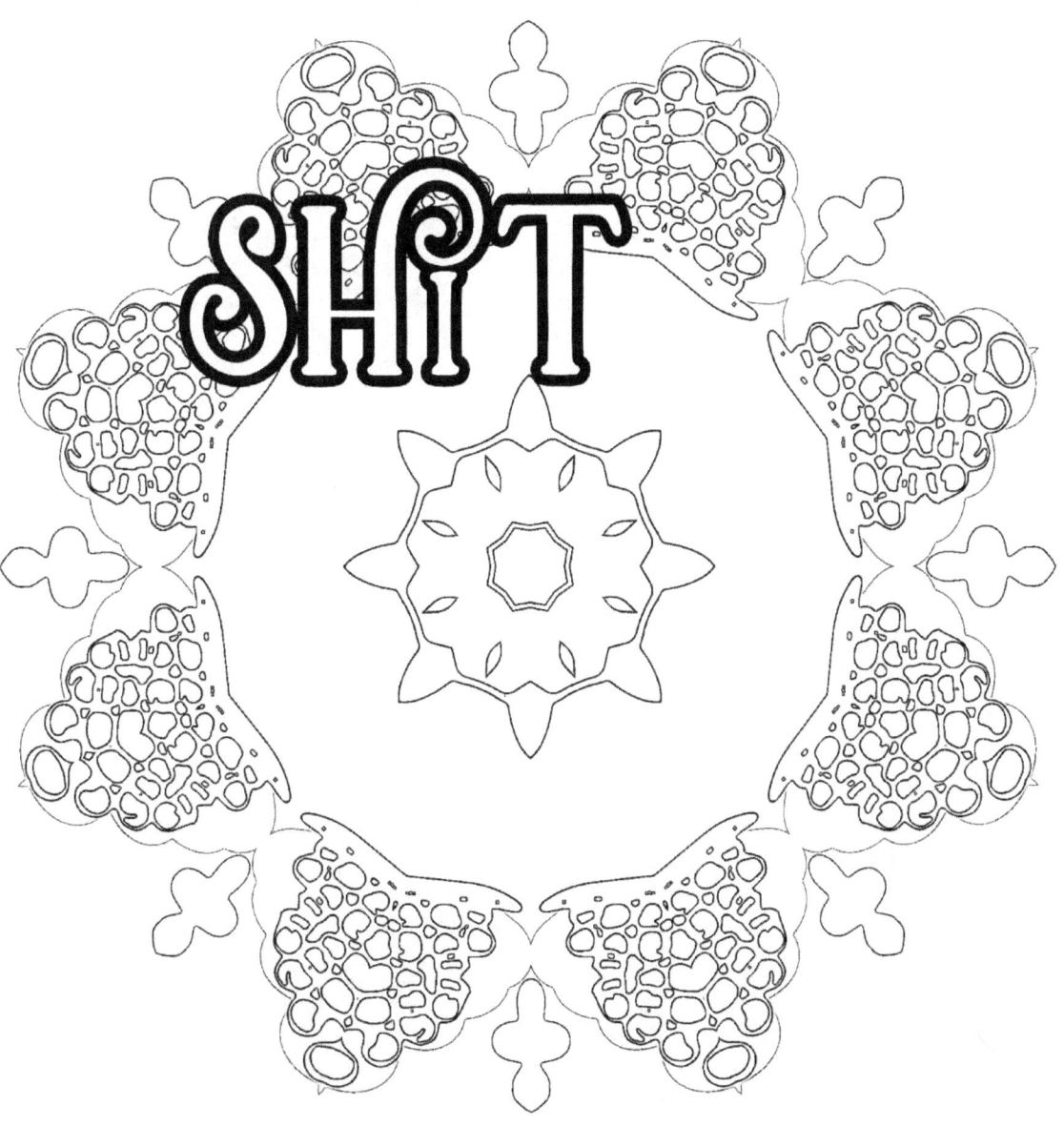

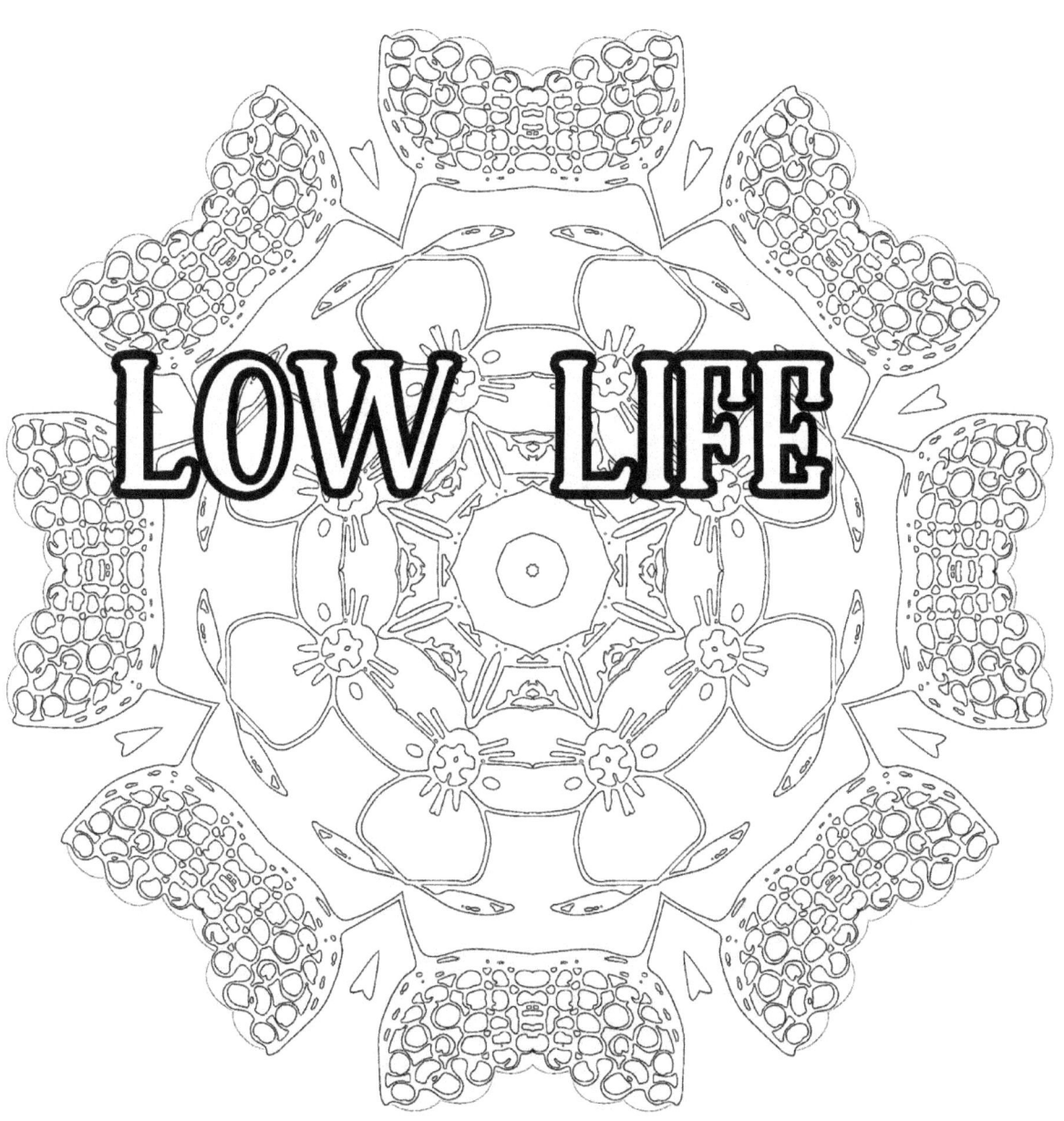

LOW LIFE

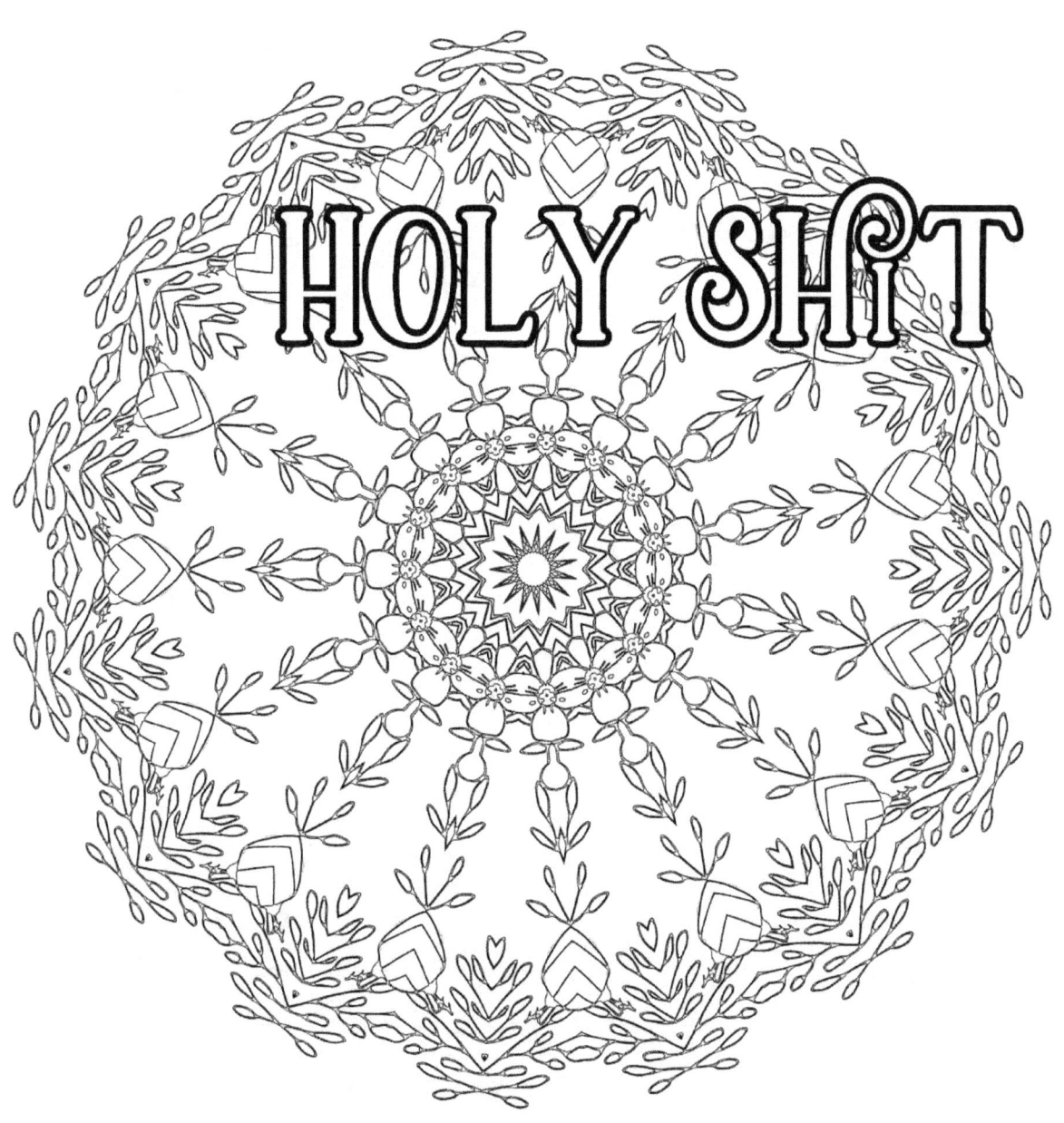

HOLY SHIT

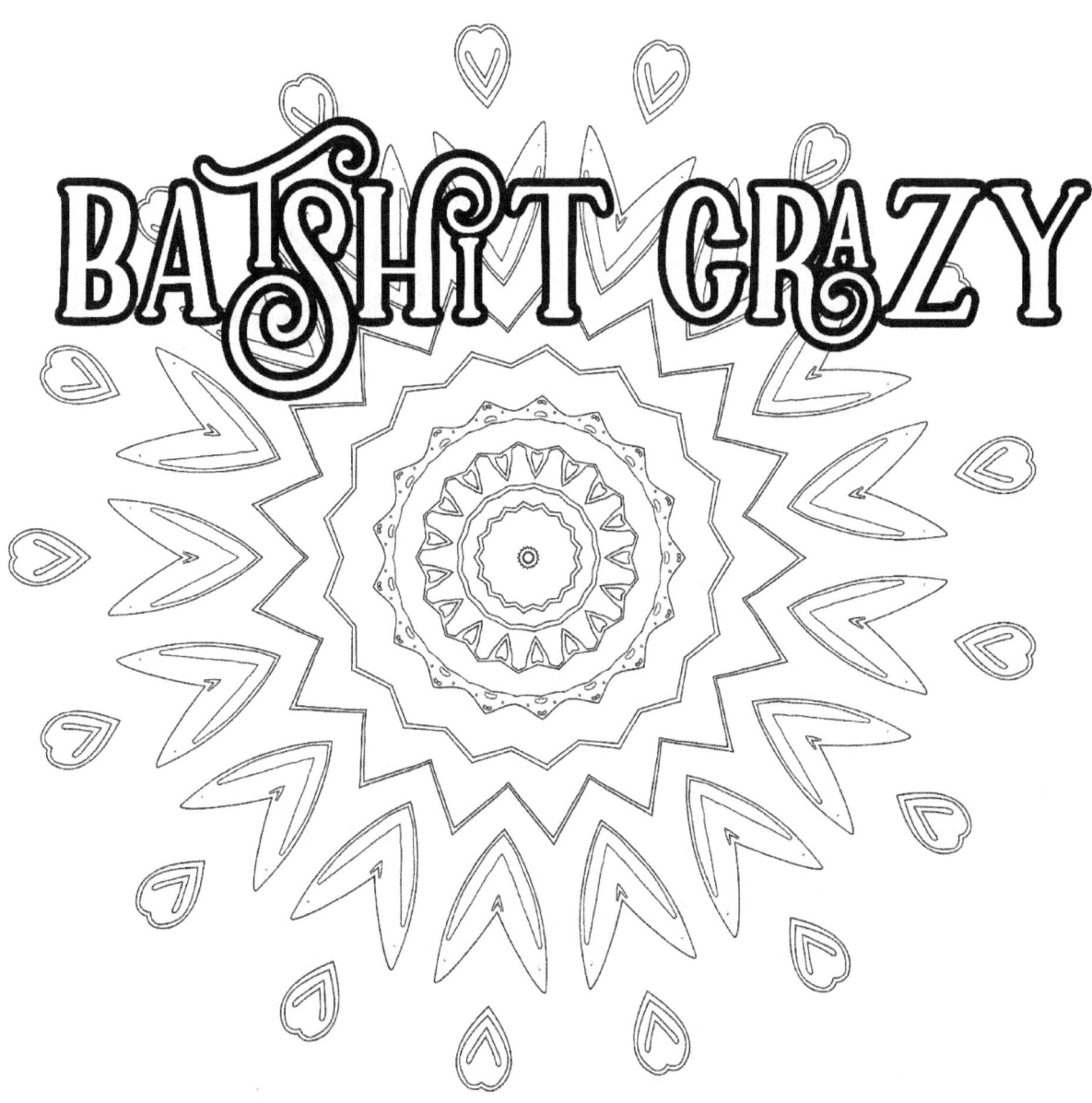

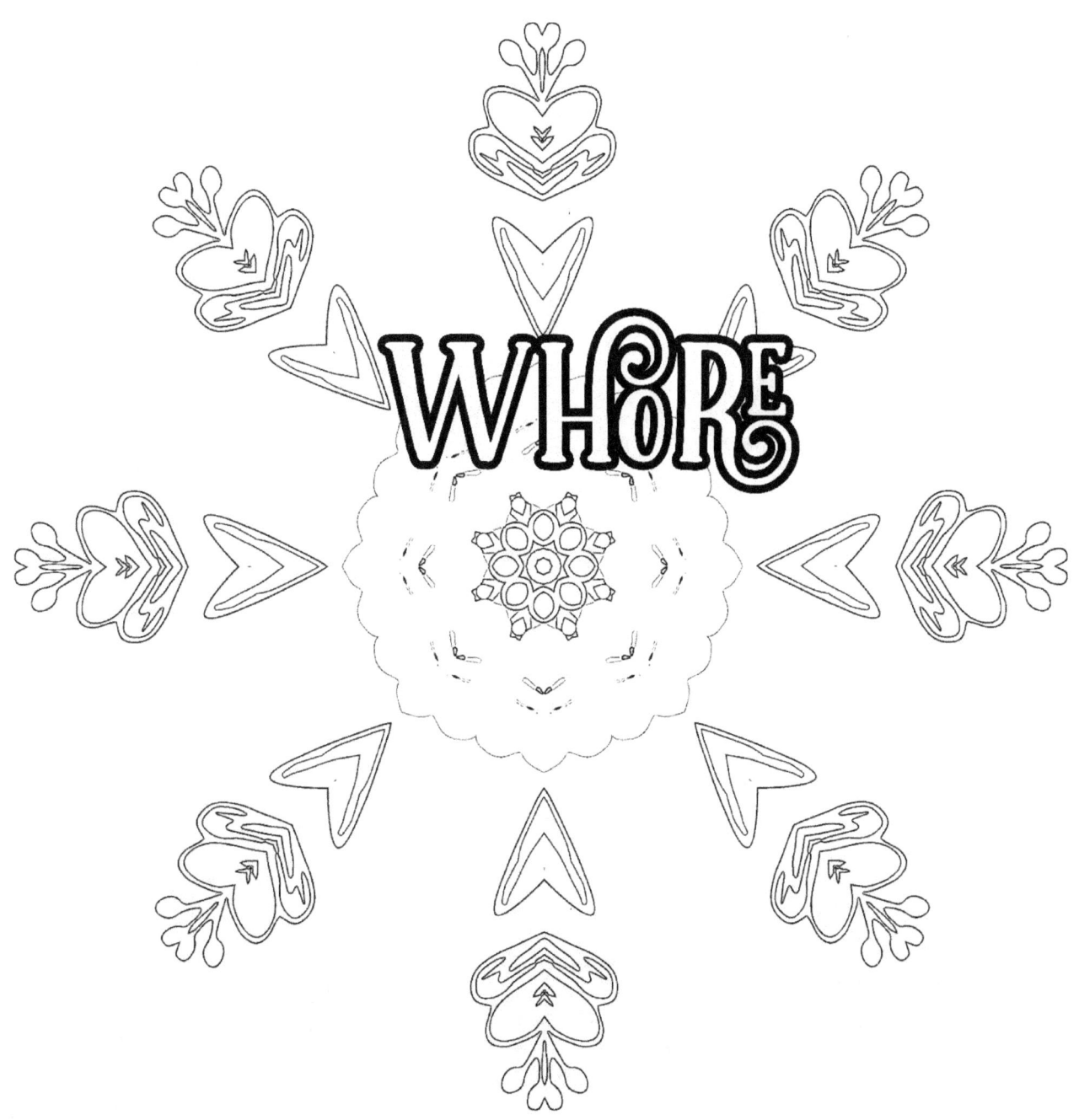

www.ingramcontent.com/pod-product-compliance
Lightning Source LLC
Chambersburg PA
CBHW081750170526
45167CB00009B/3991